# Crystalline Lifetime

*by the same author*

**Freaks, Geeks and Asperger Syndrome**
**A User Guide to Adolescence**
Luke Jackson
Foreword by Tony Attwood
ISBN 1 84310 098 3
**Winner of the NASEN & TES Special Educational Needs Children's Book Award 2003**

**A User Guide to the GF/CF Diet for Autism,**
**Asperger Syndrome and AD/HD**
Luke Jackson
With appendices by Jacqui Jackson
Foreword by Marilyn Le Breton
ISBN 1 84310 055 X

*of related interest*

**Multicoloured Mayhem**
**Parenting the many shades of adolescents**
**and children with autism, Asperger Syndrome and AD/HD**
Jacqui Jackson
ISBN 1 84310 171 8

**Asperger's Syndrome**
**A Guide for Parents and Professionals**
Tony Attwood
Foreword by Lorna Wing
ISBN 1 85302 577 1

**The Complete Guide to Asperger's Syndrome**
Tony Attwood
ISBN 1 84310 495 4

**Coming Out Asperger**
**Diagnosis, Disclosure and Self-Confidence**
Edited by Dinah Murray
ISBN 1 84310 240 4

# Crystalline Lifetime

## Fragments of Asperger Syndrome

### Luke Jackson

Jessica Kingsley Publishers
London and Philadelphia

First published in 2006
by Jessica Kingsley Publishers
116 Pentonville Road
London N1 9JB, UK
and
400 Market Street, Suite 400
Philadelphia, PA 19106, USA

**www.jkp.com**

**Library of Congress Cataloging in Publication Data**
A CIP catalog record for this book is available from the Library of Congress

**British Library Cataloguing in Publication Data**
A CIP catalogue record for this book is available from the British Library

ISBN-13: 978 1 84310 443 8
ISBN-10: 1 84310 443 1

Printed and bound in Great Britain by
Athenaeum Press, Gateshead, Tyne and Wear

# Contents

# Preface

I've heard it said before that a picture is worth a thousand words, except nobody ever says what these words are. Writing a story through pictures has long been a fascination of mine, though it has made me realize that nothing is said about the words the picture tells because the story changes and twists depending on who the viewer is – the picture is just the idea.

In the same way, when words are put together in the right way, they create images in the mind of the person browsing, a full short film that takes on the thoughts and feelings of not only the writer, but the reader.

Looking at some of the pictures and poems I'd written, I found that a lot of them fit together well, so in the pages that follow, I've included some of my own thoughts and feelings at the time of writing, in word and image form.

Signing the contract for this was the hardest job in putting together what you're about to read, as a lot of these poems are personal to me, and reflect on what I was thinking/feeling at that time.

Just note before you start to read that I've changed a lot and come a long way since I wrote these poems – I just hope that they will give you some insight into what things were like for me back then and help you to realize that life doesn't stand still.

When some of these poems were written I still attended school, and I will freely admit that life was tough.

I eventually left at the age of 14 years after completely having had enough, and I have since muddled through life, tried college and learned lots of life lessons that school prevented me from learning. I now enjoy singing and playing in a band with some mates (of whom I have many now), going out and socializing, and making new friends. The buzz of meeting new people is a far cry from the difficulties I once had – funny how things change like that. I may not always get things right but as I get older, people accept me for who I am and respect me for being myself. Kids around my age try to stand out from the crowd a lot, through fashion, music and personality, but standing out without any of this seems to come more naturally to me than most.

For those of you who have read my last book *Freaks, Geeks and Asperger's Syndrome* and have seen the (slightly outdated) picture of me on the back, I have added a newer picture of me since. I've changed a lot over the years, and to be honest, I don't even think of the spiky-haired teenager as me anymore. People have commented on how I change my appearance so drastically – I have had a shaved head, short hair, long hair, spiky hair, purple, orange and black hair and basically any colour you can think of.

This new style is one which I feel particularly comfortable with as I cover the eye that has a tendency to turn outwards – my 'squiffy eye', I guess you would call it. I am not saying do the same if you have a squiffy eye as apparently it can make the eye even lazier but for now, unless I change again, this is what I feel most confident with. After I finished school, around the age of 13 or 14, finding my identity again was hard, because expressing yourself is something that seems to be quashed in the schooling system.

The poems and photos in this book were taken over a period of around four years, so if anyone wants to ask me any questions about them and I have forgotten about them, I apologize in advance!

*Luke Jackson*

# Acknowledgements

- Mum – for being there and for all the help, and for giving me a proverbial kick up the arse to actually get this out and published.

- Anke – for giving me time to get my head round something like this, and for being so patient. I really couldn't have done this without you.

- Kyleigh – for accepting me for me, and for always being there. I love you; even though you're a loser, you're my loser.

- Jessica – for putting your trust in me and for your constant encouragement, thank you.

- For all the people that have been there for me over the past few weeks – this page isn't big enough to fit all of you in, but know that it's very much appreciated.

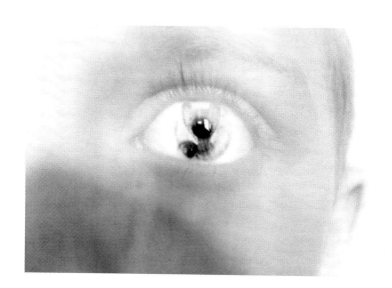

Evangelical

## *Real*

When you people look at me
What is it you think you see?
A frightened boy
Alone, afraid,
Or just a foolhardy charade?
Do you see through the shell I make?
Look closely at your empty fate;
Is this who you want to be?
A shell born of transparency?
Wake up, open your eyes,
To see the nothingness inside
A hollow shell, bereft of pride
Moulded by society, hollow
Is this the path you want to follow?

But is it true
What you think you see?
Or is it a fake?
Not the real me?
You don't know;
Probably don't care
But when you next see yourself
Beware.
Do you see yourself, real and true?
Or do you see a farce, not you?

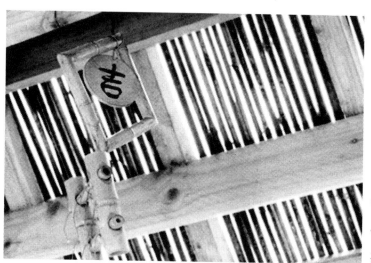

Chimes of tranquility

## *Peace*

I wonder, wandering,
Walking through the moonlit skies;
The moon rises up to meet me,
Falling through the moonlit skies.
I wonder on the origins of life,
The purpose, the universe of ethics,
The world of euphemisms we live in.
Everybody roundabout, skirting around,
Subject to forbidden subjects;
They attract us like magnets,
Bringing attraction in their revulsion.
Revolving mayhem,
And like the eye of the storm,
One stands, unchanged, unmoved,
While chaos ensues without.
The chaos without stills,
And her eyes of gold open,
As beacons of within shine brightly,
Blinding those of ill will;
While in her heart it resides.
Blinding truthfulness astride
The back of revulsion residing.
Mixing cocktails in the blender of life,
We are thrown together,
Apart from the chaos; the peace is within.
A generator of calm, the calmness spread
And together we move through the chaos.

Crystalline

# *Crystalline Lifetime*

Faceted crafting, light sparkles,
Shining through cracks and crevices,
A different image in every face,
Every geometrical square.

Light reflecting, falling through,
Seemingly random, yet chaotic
In the most orderly fashion;
Crystalline elegance, inner radiance.

Reflecting on life, passing through
and split, orderly chaotic,
Multi-faceted happenings.

Cracked faces distorting situations,
And after some time the shining,
The glistening sharpness, fades,
And blackened by time, loses its beauty
And the light cannot get through.

Sometimes the light dims before its time,
The crystal is dirtied by life,
Misgivings of society, and always
The pressure of normality.
And eventually it dies, masked;
The pressure of society's corruption.

Confused existence

# Confused

Lost my religion,
Oblivious to the oblivion,
Around me,
Do I, or do I not exist?
The tethers of humanity,
The who, why and what
Weighing us down,
All throughout history,
Always around.

What is the meaning,
Of this life we endure,
The pain, fear and anxiety,
While of what will come next,
We are always unsure,
But yet we strive on,
Through our daily activity,
Trying to exist,
Through the use of passivity.

But not for me, I cannot go on,
Through this blank life,
The veil of jobs, and work, and play,
Has gone. But what can I do,
Except go on and strive?
While the only relief
Is that none come out alive.
End the life, the pain, the strife,
Through the use of one small knife.

And then we go on,
With our pointless lives,
Defying 'the meaning'
While the pointless survives.

Strawberry fields

## *Unknown*

Dispassionate separation,
The body stays behind,
A shell of itself.
I wander, untied,
Unbound, and free
To walk where I will;
Aimlessly searching,
For something not to be,
Found, lost, misplaced,
And I lose myself,
In the everlasting moment,
Unchanging indifference,
Sameness through and
Throughout all things.
I wander in wonderment;
Lost, forgotten.
Unknown.

Potentiality

# *Release*

Taking life into my hands,
Hating you for knowing me;
Loving you,
Why did you have to make this so hard?

I wonder if you do this purposely,
Hating me,
Forsaken me, can't you see?
I'm dying.

Living the life I was born with,
Suddenly seems an impossible task,
Living, dying,
Both the same to me; I see.

If I was dying tomorrow,
Would I care to prolong my life?
Living to suffer,
Relief and release; an end.

Sundown

# Why

Ever I ask myself why,
Why this life,
That I am tortured with,
Why this death,
That I am blessed with?
Why the struggle,
That I am ever enduring?
Why the pain,
That I am always ignoring?
I ask myself why,
Through the darkness of night,
But no answer presents itself,
Lack of answers, lack of light.

By the river

# *Haze*

Haze. All-encompassing, it sits.
Waiting. For what, nobody knows;
Why? Nobody wonders.
Yet it is sentient,
Lives as human,
And thinks.

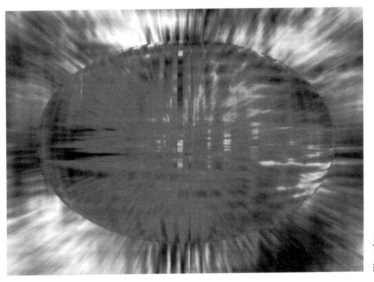

Warpsphere

## *Essence*

Poetry,
The information highway,
Speeding,
With the poetry of today,
Anticipating,
The poetry of tomorrow.
Feelings,
Pure emotion, joy and sorrow,
Realism,
Expressions of life.

Dinner and dancing

## *Knowing Inside*

Her black hair spills onto her shoulders,
Liquid midnight moonlight, black, yet silky,
And shining. Her eyes like twin pools,
The first time I saw them I was lost,
Hopelessly lost. When I saw her, I knew;
I loved her. But love is dangerous.
How could I ever be worthy of anyone like her?
Her beauty unrivalled, her full lips I long
To touch, to be near her.

So many questions, does she like me?
How would I know? Bombarding my brain,
Tainting my reality, shadowing everything
With her all-pervasive elegance
Complementing her gracious personality.
How can I tell her these feelings?
I know she won't understand. She knows,
Inwardly; I can tell. Scared;
If I do tell her, will we still be friends?

Ever I will love her,
Never she shall know.

Distant collision

## Phoenix

Her eyes like starshine,
Pure in her childlike beauty,
Unrequited love.
She has risen, above me,
While I gaze, below her.

## Cold Memories

I get goosebumps listening
To the music you make in your sleep,
It sends shivers down my spine;
Or maybe it's just cold?
Like the seeds you've sown for yourself,
They've grown to new heights,
Died at their peak.
Does that worry you?
Does me…
Least you'll never know
The sadness I felt
Listening to your brokenhearted wishsong,
And the sorrows of things
You did
Or didn't do…
A million painful 'maybes'
Strewn across the open sea.

Exchange

## The Question

It's so cold
That you can see
Your breath freeze,
In front of eyes
Squeezed shut
That look right through me.
But even though you so detest,
I see,
The way I let myself be known
Please tell me why you do so love
Living in a state of constant unrest?
Always so crowded
But never alone…
Shame you'll always hide
What was truly made just for show.

Evening light

## *Joyful Personification*

Sadness dies,
While happiness lives on.
Pain lies,
The joys tell of life's truths.
Jealousy bides,
While love waits for no man.
Anger sighs,
And returns to its birthplace.
Goodwill triumphs,
And sadness dies.
Joy fills the emptyness.

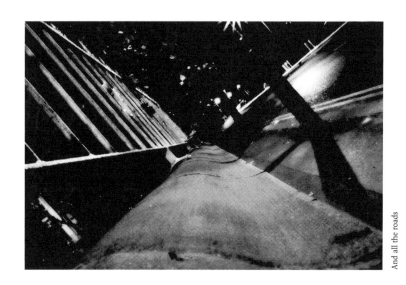

And all the roads

## *Purpose of Life*

Trying to see what wasn't there,
While others wander without a care.
With depression and anger, why am I not rife,
I know that there is no point to my life.
So why doesn't it bother me?
Why has life not yet devoured me?
I am free of depression, sadness and stress.
Suddenly life does not seem so pointless,
Deities or gods, one cannot assume,
The meaning of life, I shall now exhume.
Survival of the fittest, evolution,
There's no other purpose, no perfect solution.
Simply to live, is the purpose of life,
Through joys and happiness, pain and strife.
This scares some people, a life without purpose,
Living independently, alone in our loneliness.
We must look to each other for relief from our pain,
For only then can we be truly sane.
Sometimes God is not the answer,
For freedom from the all-pervasive cancer,
Of feelings, sadness, love, lust and hate.
With our fellow humans must we seal our own fate.
God and religion clouding our vision;
Only within humanity may we truly see.

## Commercialist Truths

Commercialism,
Blinded by everyday life,
Trapped in our routines.
The world dissolves around us,
Leaving us only the truth.

Cloudscape

# *Freak*

Freak. Freak.
All through my childhood,
The same name resonating
Through my head. Haunting me.
People treating me like mud.

Always left til the last;
Never a part of the team,
Ashamed, aside and alone.
But no, all these times
Will soon be part of the past.

No more. Above I shall rise.
A phoenix out of the ashes,
Reincarnated, yet never gone.
Above. They are below my level,
for I have touched the skies.

I am no freak.

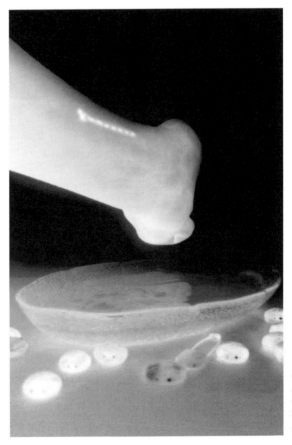

Blood is thicker than water

## Suicide Kills

Come on everybody!
Get with the trend;
It's cool to die!
(Though it's also the end.)
The last fashion,
The last fad,
Just because something made you sad?
But you chose not,
To throw the sadness away
No, you don't want to live another day.
A gun, a noose, a knife, some pills,
But kids,
Just remember this:
Suicide kills.

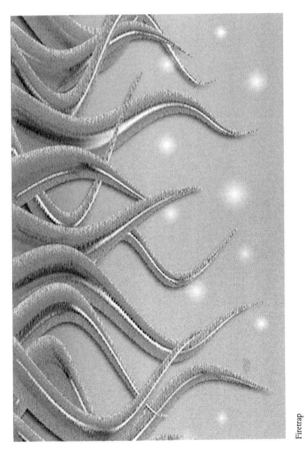

Firetrap

## The Dragons Fly

The dragons fly.
Twisting acrobatically;
Swirling. Like moving mist,
They soar. Defying gravity;
Pushing their way through
The immaterial clouds.

The dragons fly.
This time;
It may be their last.
They have come to take them,
And their fiery, vengeful breath,
Is ineffectual. Dark shadows,
Twisting, swirling. And then –
They are gone. All is quiet.

The dragons fly once more.

Beauty

# Cherry Blossoms

Twisting and turning,
Wriggling, writhing out of reach,
What are these I see?
Cherry blossoms on the wind,
Nature reaching out to me.

Caged

## Possibilities

Trying to hold on,
A spanner in the works,
Living for the good times,
While all the time I hurt.
Remembering the many joys,
When not before so long,
Just when things all seemed ok,
Everything went horribly wrong.
Then life didn't seem so easy.
Things just didn't flow.
I had to find out what went bad,
Shrivelled fruit left out to rot,
The mouldy wreck I had to show.
A spanner in the works,
Though what the spanner was,
I really didn't know.
Behind my back it lurked,
Just beyond my grasp,
I guess I should have known,
That the good times wouldn't last.

But then things change;
The difficulties, while not gone,
Can be endured. And through the stress,
I remember, that life is worth living.
We can make it through this.

Anything is possible.

Liquified technicalities

## Liquid Existence

Times of happiness,
Running like water, giving
Life to beholders.
Irretrievable silver,
Joyful, pure liquid moonlight.

Noughts and crosses

# *Fleeting Moments*

Happiness.
The fleeting moments,
Making life worth living.
Always gone so quickly,
Yet the memory stays.
The good times outweighing
The bad, if not through quantity,
Through experience.
The memory stays.

Cool ice

## Belittled Burdens

I'm hot and I'm cold
I'm numb but I'm not
I'm feeling these feelings
All of which I thought that I'd forgotten
And will you please tell me
Is this good or bad

Bad to the bone?
Or rotten to the core
Just like the apple that you
Shot off of the top of my head
Piercing my soul.

First uncaring, unmeaning, now
Filled with these thoughts of you
Did you miss me?
Guess not, guess so…

Guess all these feelings I'm feeling
Feeling when I am with you
There's nothing you could do
To make me unhappy.

Your words feel like kisses
These razorblades against my lips
Make me feel everything is just right
Just here, just now
It's just that now and again
It feels like I'm just floating
Here with you…

Everything goes up
Must come down sometime
And you know time goes by
Faster than it should
So hold your head up
Don't look down, look to the sky
And remember me when I'm gone.

LIVE FOR LIFE

THE PRESENT IS A GIFT ONLY GRANTED ONCE.

# Little Somethings

Strange how some people can turn up
The corners of your mouth so easily
How they can make you feel warm in an iceberg
As easy as putting on a jacket is to you and me
And it's a funny thing
How I keep wondering
If all your little somethings
Are so easy to see
Maybe to passers-by, you don't shine so brightly?
Sometimes I want to make them notice
See you like I do
Make them feel like I do around you
It's a funny thing
Feeling like everything is okay
Being able to be myself around you
But mostly, it's funny,
Knowing that everything I write here is true.

Pyramid of Isis

## *Stranger and Strangers*

A rolling stone gathers no moss
'cept issues lost in times gone by
When we used to sit all alone
Wondering whether we'll ever
Find the light again
Belittling big issues
And compressing problems
To turn our backs on our burdens
Now life just seems heavy
Like one great sigh
Passed from the lips of a dying man
To a world long dead…
Long gone
Passed away
And turned to better days
To forget those left behind
And mourn passing strangers.

Rainbow

# *Nothing Means Nothing Anymore*

A stone dropped in water
Makes ripples all around
Your words create craters
The lake's all dried up
You say you're torn between us
I'm torn and broken
Torn between truth and lies
And neverending sacrifice
You ask what's wrong…
'Nothing.'
Means nothing anymore.

So after all is said and done
And all these little somethings
Become one
A huge gaping hole
A glaring eye
Staring out my soul…
Something's wrong
Something is missing
Something's out of place
You ask me what's right…

All I can answer is…
'Nothing.'
Means nothing anymore.

Peace offering

## Love Answered

I asked a simple question
Full of so many complicated answers
Entwining and twisting out of reach;
'Are you real?'
Love answered: 'I'm as real as the teardrop
Rolling down your cheek;
Your last kiss in the rain…
Even though you know for sure
It's going to be the last time you'll meet.
So don't ask me if I am real;
Don't ask me if it's true what you heard
What you see, what you feel
Can be written down in one little word…
Just ask:
Are you true to yourself?
And if you can say 'yes'
And you can mean that one syllable
Then your answer can be heard
On the winds of change
And your lover's kiss.

Timeless

# All That's Left, Seeming Right

When the whole world expects from you
What you don't expect from yourself
What else is there to do but watch and wait?
To sit back
Enjoy the show
Accept your fate and take control
Of the chances and certain subtleties
That make life worthwhile and worth living
Just because you care about nothing
And everything but yourself and anyone else
All the while all there is to do
Is to sing of the troubles
And the times you left behind you
All you can see is left drained and stained
With the awkward silences you thought you knew
The whole world upside down
Askew and alone
And all there is in the dark corner of your mind is…
You.

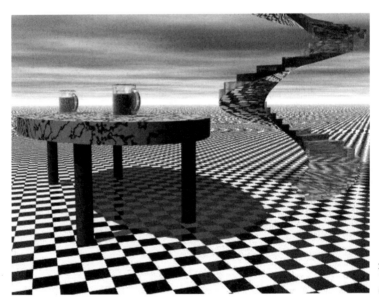

Beer table

## Said the Wimble to the Wimbles

Said the Wimble Wee
To the Wimbles three,
'I cannot see without you,'
Said the Wimbles three
To the Wimble Wee
'My dear,
I guess you'll have to.
For we need ourselves
To see, you see,
And sail in seas
All full of trees
Of leaves
And sprigs of Wimble things.'
So the Wimble Wee
Walked on by
Quite sadly;
For without the Wimbles three
He could not see, you see.

Turmoil in a glass

# Murderer

Insomnia;
The highlight of my night.
Late night walks down the street.
I see a pub brawl going on somewhere,
A drunken, sprawling fight,
Unto death,
Or something like it.
Hungover and headachy,
Feelin' like shit,
They head home,
Stopping on the way to mug yours truly.
'10p? That it?
That all you got?'
'Spent most to get some fags, see,
Then threw the rest down a drain, see.'
'What you go and do that for?'
'Boredom, see –
You want to have a go at being me
Just for a day, maybe,
To see how boredom can kill you.
Could kill me.
Anything to stay amused,
Whispering sweet nothings to ease the mind...
Anyway, gonna have to flee;
I got nothing to do,
No people to see.'
And with that, I walked on home,
A trail of 10ps left behind.

## Defining Gravity

Defining Gravity was a challenging series of shots, conceptually and photographically. At first, the concept of the shots was to freeze time, defy gravity, but then I went one further — what happened when the laws of gravity were first written? Was the apple that brought about the discovery of gravity shown how to fall, which way, and how fast?

I'm obviously only speaking metaphorically here but think about the principles of gravity, or what we know of it. While I'm no physicist there seem to be a lot of laws and doctrines that are unchanging and only vary with the object falling.

So, then we go back to 'defining gravity', in short, 'teaching the apple how to fall'. What if things weren't so simple and didn't go the way they were supposed to, or at the right speed, or simply didn't move at all?

With that in mind I started on these photographs, deciding to illustrate the different shortfalls of gravity — cryokinesis, the ability to manipulate ice, and levitation, put simply, the ability to make things float.

Photographically, these were both difficult photos; when a shutter is only opened for a very short amount of time, a small fraction of a second, the film (or digital equivalent thereof) is exposed to only a tiny amount of light, and this has the effect of freezing the subject, in this case water, or a spoon.

More than anything though, these photos were possibly the most fun to take out of all the shots in this book; Levitation basically had me looking like a complete idiot throwing spoons up in the air in front of a camera, and as for Cryokinesis...well, the picture was taken in the bathroom around mid-evening, and I think it took me pretty much the rest of the night to mop up the water and even longer to get myself dry!

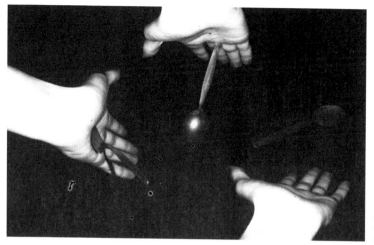

Levitation

Cryokinesis

# *Painting with Light*

To be honest, this series came about purely because light is something that always has and always will fascinated me – the way different substances break it up into different wave lengths, the way it varies with the way it's generated, and so on.

Light has always interested me – when I was a child my room was full of lights, lava lamps, lightning balls, the works – but I think the real fascination stemmed from when I was a kid in primary school, when I was around eight. We were doing an experiment, shining light from a bulb, and we used a few small mirrors to direct it better, through a triangular prism onto a piece of white paper. Before the experiment, none of the class knew what to expect, but the subsequent rainbow amazed me – how could so many colors be hidden in the dim light the bulb shone, how could a rainbow be created from a set-up so small?

Later on this led to my love of photography, the art of capturing light, trapping it and putting it down onto other media, first photo paper in black and white, then a computer screen through digital photography, basically, 'painting with light'.

But, in photography, darkness, or lack of the palette the photographer commands (or more often than not, simply captures) is just as important. Think of silhouettes, shadows, and other such apparitions so important in taking pictures. In short, 'painting with darkness', manipulating the shadows, is just as important as painting with light.

To those confused, the first picture, 'Painting With Darkness', is simply natural sunlight hitting water droplets on a DVD against a plain background. The second, 'Painting With Light' was a little more complicated – it was a long exposure shot (a method of photography where the shutter on a camera is left open for an extended period of time) of a plasma ball with a small decorative model in front, again over a plain background.

However, things don't always turn out as they seem, and I'll let you work out the differences in these photomanipulations – it shouldn't be too hard.

Painting with darkness

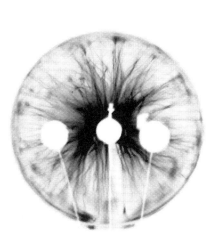

Painting with light

# *Repetition*

The Repetition series came about when I was idly looking for more ideas and inspiration for photos, and it came to me that there is a startling amount of repetition within our society and daily life in general, particularly in nature. Think of the obvious examples of leaves on trees, the trees themselves, how the general structure and make-up is similar even throughout the various species and subspecies, and you'll notice things around you immediately. It is as if someone thought, 'This works, so let's keep it like this'.

It appears that people find repetition, along with symmetry, to be somewhat comforting in the chaos of their daily rituals; think of cars on a road, benches in a park, and windows in a house. In design, repetition is obviously used for colour and general composition, but is it just that? To me, repetition some-times seems to be a comfort blanket – a means of feeling secure more than anything else.

This need for sameness and consistency may be one of the reasons why 'aspies' offend some people simply with their exis-tence. Imagine a red brick wall, stretching as far as the eye can see, then picture one or two bricks painted a bright, luminous blue. They stand out, and a lot of people don't like that, a fact which never ceases to puzzle me given that it is people on the autistic spectrum who are supposed to be somewhat inflexible.

It also never ceases to amuse me that society in general seems to have developed an autism-like rigidity...before you laugh, think about it carefully if you have difficulty picturing it. Imagine a primary school playground, all the kids in lines and all in the same school uniform. Each child follows virtually the same syllabus and if a child has special needs, they may have an 'indi-vidual programme' but this also follows the rules of the Local Education Authority and fits within the school guidelines so it is hardly individual! It sounds a little scary put like that, doesn't it?

While I may have gone off on a tangent a little bit, the talk about anomalies and people and things standing out wasn't completely unrelated. See if you can spot any in a few of the photos...

Repetition – fascination

Repetition – indulgence

Repetition – life

Repetition – power

Repetition – technology

Repetition – vanity